HORRIBLE SCIENCE

TEACHERS' RESOURCES

LIGHT

Nick Arnold • Tony De Saulles

additional material David Tomlinson

AUTHOR
Nick Arnold

ILLUSTRATIONS
Tony De Saulles

ADDITIONAL MATERIAL
David Tomlinson

EDITOR
Wendy Tse

ASSISTANT EDITOR
Charlotte Ronalds

SERIES DESIGNER
Joy Monkhouse

DESIGNERS
Joy Monkhouse
Catherine Mason

This book contains extracts from *Frightening Light, Suffering Scientists, Explosive Experiments* and *Killer Scientists* in the Horrible Science series. Text © 1999, 2000, 2001, 2001 Nick Arnold.
Illustrations © 1999, 2000, 2001, 2001 Tony De Saulles.
First published by Scholastic Children's Books.
Additional text © 2005, David Tomlinson.

Published by Scholastic Ltd
Villiers House
Clarendon Avenue
Leamington Spa
Warwickshire
CV32 5PR

www.scholastic.co.uk

Printed by Bell & Bain Ltd, Glasgow

1 2 3 4 5 6 7 8 9   5 6 7 8 9 0 1 2 3 4

British Library Cataloguing-in-Publication Data

WELL, THAT'S BRIGHTENED UP MY DAY!

A catalogue record for this book is available from the British Library.

ISBN 0-439-97190-X
ISBN 978-0439-97190-4
The right of David Tomlinson to be identified as the Author of additional text of this Work has been asserted by him in accordance with the Copyright, Designs and Patents Act 1988.

TEACHERS' NOTES

Horrible Science: Teachers' Resources: Light is inspired by the Horrible Science book *Frightening Light*. Each photocopiable page takes a weird and wonderful excerpt from the original, as well as material from *Killer Energy*, *Suffering Scientists* and *Explosive Experiments*, and expands on it to create a class-based teaching activity, fulfilling both National Curriculum and QCA objectives. The activities can be used individually or in a series as part of your scheme of work.

With an emphasis on research, experimentation and interpreting results, the activities will appeal to anyone even remotely curious about the Horrible world around us!

PART 1:
LOOKING AT LIGHT

Page 11: Gruesome gloom
Learning objective
Light travels from a source.
That there are many light sources and light is needed to see.

Start this session by inviting your class to look around them. Ask them what they can see and how it is that they are able to see these things. Guide the discussion to situations where we cannot see or can only see partially. What is missing that would enable us to see well? Challenge the children to list things that rely on natural light (such as plants) as well as those that rely on light generated by electricity (such as television). Use their ideas as the basis for a story imagining a world without light. Use the cartoon on photocopiable page 11 as a starting point and ask the children what they think is happening to the people calling out in the cartoon.

Page 12: Seeing the light
Learning objective
Light travels from a source.
Light cannot pass through some materials; this leads to the formation of shadows.

Use photocopiable page 12 as the start of a session looking at light and shadow. Split your class into detective groups and tell them that all the clues are on the photocopiable page. Equip each group with a torch, a pair of scissors and a piece of card. Encourage the groups to use these detection tools to unravel the mystery. They can cut out the figure of the

man on the sheet, shine the torch and see a shadow form on the cardboard; some children will need more teacher-led clues than others. Bring the detective groups together at the end of the session to discuss findings and solutions.
Answer: DON'T PANIC! As the scientist realised, the figure was only his own shadow. This very real if ghostly effect is called the spectre of the Brocken after the Brocken Mountain in Germany where it's often seen. If you climb a mountain near sunset (not a very safe thing to do – so don't try it on your own) the low sun can cast your shadow on nearby clouds. And you see a huge ghostly figure.

THIS IS AN 'ARROWING EXPERIENCE!

Page 13: Lovely light sources
Learning objective
That there are many light sources and light is needed to see.
We see things when light enters our eyes.

This activity takes a closer look at the light sources we use today and puts them in a historical perspective. Start the session by teaching by candlelight only, asking the children to work out how a candle works (warn the children about using candles unsupervised). Recap any work you may have done about solids and liquids, encouraging the children to apply scientific language to what they observe. Focus on the way we use light today, explaining that over time we have developed different ways of using light. For example: early man used flint to make a spark; the invention of matches in the 1850s; the development of gas light, electricity, lasers, and so on. Use photocopiable page 13 to record these discoveries in a timeline, which can be the basis of a class display.

Bonus Investigation Answer: CD players use a laser to 'read' what is on the disc, taking the place of the needle on old gramophones. The laser flickers as it reflects off a pattern of pits on the surface of the CD. The CD player turns this flicker into electric pulses and processes this into music.

Page 14: Sunny day at Stonehenge
Learning objective
Light cannot pass through some materials. Shadows are formed by blocked light and that these can be measured for data.

Start this session by asking the children to imagine what would happen if all the watches and clocks in the world stopped. Ask them how we could still tell the time. How would we know it was morning or time to go to bed? Focus on how our days and years are based on the movements of the sun and Earth. Use photocopiable page 14 to introduce the idea of measurement using sun and shadows. Encourage the children to measure carefully during this activity and to share their findings. Use a compass to focus your class on the direction in which the sun rises and sets, and encourage them to design their own sundials for a class display.

Page 15: A daring discovery
Learning objective
To think creatively in order to try and explain how living and non-living things work, and to establish links between causes and effects.
To use a wide range of methods including fair testing.

Recap any work you may have done with your class about angles. Using a torch, establish the principle that light travels in a straight line. Explain that we can manipulate the angles that light can be deflected. Then introduce the activity on photocopiable page 15, focusing on the basic principle of fair testing.
Answers: 1 c) The light bounces (reflects) off the underside of the water. The surface of the water is

very smooth and the photons of light can all reflect in the same direction.
2 a) Light doesn't always go in a straight line. When light travels from air to water it slows to 224,900km per second. This is because the photons have to push through lots of atoms in the water – just imagine a crowd of people trying to run through another crowd. When a beam of light hits the water at an angle one side of the beam slows before the other. This makes the beam bend, an effect known as refraction.

Page 16: The eyes have it!
Learning objective
We see things when light enters our eyes.

Start this session with a game of 'Blind Man's Bluff' to focus the children on their eyes and how they use them. Ask them how they think they can see. Commonly they will believe they see out of their eyes, whereas it is light entering their eyes that makes vision possible. Use photocopiable page 16 to look more closely at this – enlarging it to A3 size will allow for pairs or groups to cut out and match the labels. Encourage group discussions to work out what each part of the eye does and compare answers. Be prepared to join in discussing and, if necessary, prompt the children to identify the parts. The coin experiment is a good extension activity but should be used selectively if you have any children with restricted sight in your class.
Answers: 1 Ciliary muscles. **2** Iris. **3** Optic nerve. **4** Retina with rod and cone cells. **5** Cornea. **6** Eyelashes. **7** Lens. **8** Watery bit. **9** Sclera (sk-leer-a). **10** Eye muscles. **1 g) 2 d)** Light goes through the pupil – the hole in the middle. (The colour of your eye doesn't make any difference to what you see.) **3 i)** They're nerve fibres. Their job is to take the pattern of light signals picked up by the retina to the brain in the form of nerve signals. **4 e)** It's got seven million cone cells to give you colour vision and 130 million rod cells that detect light but not colours. **5 h)** The cornea has no blood vessels to supply it with the sugar and oxygen it needs to stay alive. It gets sugars from the gloopy fluid in the eye and oxygen directly from the air. **6 a)** They fall out after three months, but you always grow more. **7 f)** The lens thickens or lengthens so that light from whatever you are looking at is bent (refracted) and so focused on the retina. **8 b)** Yes, it's true, you're looking at this page through a pool of watery jelly. **9 j)** It's the

'white' of your eyeball. When the eyeball is injured or has a disease the blood vessels get inflamed and get bigger. And the eyeball looks gungey and bloodshot. **10 c)** They also swivel the eyeball round to look at things. Your brain coordinates the muscles on each eyeball so they work together. When this doesn't happen you go cross-eyed.

Page 17: A handy illusion
Learning objective
Light enters our eyes enabling us to see.

The activity on photocopiable page 17 is designed to follow on from any work you may have done about how the eye works, putting two images together to form a whole. Start by asking the children to join the tips of their index fingers and position them horizontally about 30cm from their eyes, slowly bringing them closer. Ask them to describe the illusion that develops (eventually the two index fingers look like a string of sausages). Tell any children who are struggling to see the sausages to focus on something behind their fingers, as this will relax their eyes. Use this and the activity on photocopiable page 17 as the basis for a class gallery of optical illusions (you could include pictures by M.C. Escher or Magic Eye illusions, for example).
Answer: b) Your left and your right eyes are seeing different views. Your brain combines them to make a three-dimensional scene. This is what happens all the time when you look at things but in this case the scene is a rather horrible illusion.

Pages 18 & 19: The awesome eclipse show! 1 & 2
Learning objective
That the position of the sun changes.
To know that shadows form when light is blocked.
To think creatively in order to try and explain how living and non-living things work, and to establish links between causes and effects.

Use the stories and cartoons on photocopiable page 19 as the basis for your own awesome eclipse show. Photocopiable page 20 models how to start a script and adapt the stories into short scenes or sketches. Use the script to encourage the children to act confidently. Next, get your class to talk about their own drama ideas, starting with improvisation and working up to writing their own scripts. Use children to play the parts of planets (remember that torches are required for the sun!) and challenge the audience to vote for the story that they think explains the phenomenon most scientifically.

Page 20: The awesome eclipse show! 3
Learning objective
To think creatively in order to try and explain how living and non-living things work, and to establish links between causes and effects.
Light cannot pass through some materials; this leads to the formation of shadows.

This activity can be used to follow on from photocopiable pages 18 and 19 or you can adapt a favourite class story/film/class-written tale for a shadow-theatre show. Challenge your class to solve the mystery on photocopiable page 20 and to design dramatic and effective puppets. A common mistake is to draw on the puppets or add detail within the shape that will not show up in silhouette; use this as an opportunity to talk about shadows and how they are formed and can be manipulated.
Answer: b) When the shape is closer to the light, it blocks more light. This throws a larger shadow on the wall. The larger shadow has more of a blurred edge than the smaller one. This is because some light from the edges of the torch can still shine past the edges of the shape, but not enough to give a sharp edge to the shadow.

Page 21: The glow-in-the-dark zoo!
Learning objective
We see when light enters our eyes.
To use a wide range of methods for research.

Start this session by drawing the curtains and switching off any lights. Prepare one child to enter the classroom wearing a scary glow-in-the-dark mask. After the initial reaction, ask the children what they can see and why they think this is. Switch on the lights and make a list of things that they have seen which also glow in the dark (gel pens, for example). Use photocopiable page 21 to widen the discussion to look at living and non-living examples and classify them for a class display. Continue the spooky theme from your introduction with the final activity on the sheet!

Answer: c) Before new cemeteries were opened up in Victorian times many old churchyards became full up. Dead bodies were buried one on top of the other under a shallow layer of soil. Germs inside the rotting bodies made methane and phosphine (foz-feen) gas. As the gases reached the surface they often caught fire as a result of chemical reactions with oxygen in the air. The result was a pale blue glow that was called a will o' the wisp.

Page 22: Awful advertising
Learning objective
There are many light sources.
To use observations to draw conclusions.

Start this session by asking your class why they chose certain trainers or crisps or any of their recent purchases. Focus the children on advertising and how it is used to promote certain properties of an item (for example, an advert will stress that football boots have good grip and aid ball control). Apply this consumerist know-how to different types of light. Use photocopiable page 22 to show print adverts and challenge your class to use them as the basis for television adverts, adding other light sources (such as lasers). Perform the advert for a neighbouring class, explaining that each individual has enough money for two light sources. Count up the choices afterwards and use the results for a class graph.

Page 23: Brighter bulbs
Learning objective
To make and record observations.
To use observations to draw conclusions.

Start this session by switching on a torch with a blown bulb and asking the class what reasons there might be for the torch not working. Test the batteries on another torch to establish in front of your class that the power source is not the problem.

When the children suggest it is the bulb ask them to explain this. Invite a pair of children to look at a clear working bulb with its filament intact, and at another that is not working and to compare them. Note any observations. Use photocopiable page 23 to focus your class on looking closely at the bulbs and identifying different parts. Compare differently sized and shaped bulbs, concentrating on what they have in common, for example filaments and wires, and encourage the children to use these common factors as labels for their diagram. Recap any work you may have done on electricity. Widen the debate to include different bulbs for different jobs, the amount of light required in different situations, and so on. Use the finished photocopiables as the basis to make a 3-D bulb model as part of a display.

═══════ **PART 2:** ═══════
MIRRORS, COLOUR AND REFRACTION

Page 24: Miraculous mirrors 1
Learning objective
To use descriptions involving a sequence of events to understand reflection.

Start this session by letting each child examine a selection of mirrors and ask them what they see. Establish what mirrors are and what we use them for (vanity, driving safely, and so on). Use photocopiable page 24 to focus the children on true and false ideas about mirrors, extending it by asking them to pose their own questions. Use these to expand the quiz element of the photocopiable, then collate all of the questions and use them in a class quiz book for visitors.

Page 25: Miraculous mirrors 2
Learning objective
To describe the sequence of events involved in reflection.
To understand that light is reflected from surfaces.

Recap any work you may have done about mirrors and their uses, using photocopiable page 25 to focus your class on the concept that a mirror image is the 'wrong' way around (things are shown opposite to how they really are). Encourage the children to use their mirrors to work out the answers themselves before using the mirror to decode the answer box. Encourage the use of the words 'symmetrical' and 'non-symmetrical' when comparing the mirror drawings. Use them for an interactive display, complete with mirror-written captions.

Page 26: Murderous mirrors!
Learning objective
To describe the sequence of events for reflection.
To understand that light is reflected from surfaces.

Start this session by reading the gruesome stories on photocopiable page 26 together as a class. Talk about the different ways in which mirrors have been used. Split the children into investigation groups and challenge them to recreate the story of the Greeks and Romans from the sheet. Ask the groups to consider what equipment they will need and how they can use it. Encourage trial and error, and focus the children in the latter stages of the re-enactment to use protractors to measure the angle they need to hold the mirrors at to score a light 'hit' on the boats. Ask your investigative teams to come together at the end and to share their findings.

Page 27: Surprising spoons
Learning objective
To describe reflection.
To understand that light is reflected from surfaces.

Start this session by talking about any experiences the children may have of visiting a hall of mirrors. Add any observations your class may have of 'odd' reflections distorting an image (such as a puddle or reflection of a car window). Use photocopiable page 27 to focus your class on observing differences

and noting them accurately. It may be useful to use separate blank sheets of paper to draw the reflections in detail. Encourage the children to work in pairs and to compare their answers at the end of the session. Also encourage the general use of the terms 'convex' and 'concave' and use the drawings as the basis of a hall-of-mirrors display.

Page 28: The Mystery of Mirror Mansion
Learning objective
To describe the sequence of events for reflection.
To understand that light travels.
To understand that light is reflected from surfaces.

Start this session by reading a short ghost story or poem. Talk to the children about their favourite ghost stories, movies and television shows, explaining that although some people do believe in the existence of ghosts most do not. Discuss how film makers use special effects to create a memorable ghost for an audience and that they may use lighting effects and mirrors in order to achieve the desired result. Use photocopiable page 28 to try out one such method. Encourage the children to try out their own variations on the instructions in a trial and error session. Use the story planner to link to any work you may have done about story writing and encourage the children to read their stories with full ghostly effects!
Answer: b) The lines and the paper are non-reflective. Their atoms soak up the light from the torch. This means there are areas of the mirror's reflection that appear dark and this is what you see.

Pages 29 & 30: Ridiculous refraction 1 & 2
Learning objective
To understand that light beams travel.
To understand that light travels from a source.

Start this session by looking at photocopiable page 29 and the collection of different objects drawn on the sheet. Discuss what they have in common and then focus your class on a tank with three bright objects (representing the fish mentioned on the photocopiable). Ask the children how many objects they can see. Add water and talk to them about the refraction they may observe from an upper angle. Use a copy of Henri Matisse's 'Goldfish', which perfectly captures refraction at work, to illustrate this point.

Emphasise that there are still three objects in the tank and that the illusion of six is the result of refraction. Encourage your class to record their observations and to add or take away and reposition the objects in the tank to see if these variables make a difference. If you have a sink then use photocopiable page 30 as an extension; alternatively it can be a useful homework exercise.

Answer: c) The water bent the light towards you so the coin appeared closer. As the water drained away the light refracted less. The coin appeared to move away until it disappeared behind the rim. But actually the coin didn't move.

Page 31: Crucial colours
Learning objective
To make systematic observations.

Start this session by looking at the colours in the classroom. Challenge the children to work in groups to list as many as they can in just five minutes. Bring the colour lists together and count up how many were observed. Use photocopiable page 31 to introduce the idea that light has a role to play in the colours we perceive. Do the experiment in groups or pairs, comparing results later. Encourage your class to record the experiment in their own words.

Answer: a) White paper reflects all the colours of light that fall on it. The pink glow is due to the red light reflecting off the tomato and on to the paper. All the other colours in the light get soaked up by the tomato. The experiment proves that colours are indeed caused by the reflection of light.

Page 32: Mysterious mixing
Learning objective
To make systematic observations.
To review work and that of others to describe its significance.

Start this session by looking at a collection of photographs, a mixture of colour and black and white (history books will have plenty of examples of the latter). Ask the children to sort them without giving them any criteria. See what criteria they choose in groups and discuss the difference between colour and black and white. Use photocopiable page 32 to introduce the idea that not every creature sees things

the same way and that some animals see in black and white all the time. Use the activity to encourage the children to imagine seeing the world in black and white, and to compare their observations. You can extend this to become a class display, contrasting human, cat, and squid vision!

Page 33: Colour vision!
Learning objective
To make systematic observations.
To review work and that of others to describe its significance.

Use photocopiable page 33 to continue any work you may have done on colour and light. Start with paints to try and make the colour black, as detailed on the photocopiable sheet, talking through each stage and the role that light has to play. Try out the Dare you discover activity, encouraging the children to discuss their theories confidently.

Answer: c) Your eye sees yellow by firing green and red cone cells. Your brain mixes these sensations to make yellow. But after a while the cells become less sensitive. Meanwhile blue cone cells are still firing in this area of your retina so you see a blue image. You see 'after-images' for the same reason. Mind you – it took a few disgusting eyeball experiments before scientists worked this out.

PART 3:
TRAVELLING LIGHT AND LASERS

Page 34: Laser maths!
Learning objective
To understand that light beams travel.
To consider a range of sources of information to answer questions.

Start this session by recapping any work you may have done using decimals. Use photocopiable page 34 to introduce the concept that light travels and that this journey can be measured in terms of time and distance. Relate this to the children's experiences of their own journeys and make a list of a few examples of these. Then use this data to work out the average speed that they were travelling at. Focus your class on the information about light travel on the photocopiable, and encourage them to use the data to work out the speed of light and to contrast that with human speeds. Use books and the internet and also books of records to compare fast animals, rockets and so on with light. Encourage your class to make up their own questions on this theme for a class quiz. **Answers: 1)** 0.42 seconds. **2)** 1.25 seconds. **3)** The figure given for the distance to the moon is within its orbital range and it produces the correct result; therefore the laser's light travels at 299,792km per second.

Page 35: Laser hall of fame!
Learning objective
To understand that light beams travel from a source.
To consider a range of sources of information to answer questions.

Start by talking about the characters in the *Star Wars* movies and their 'light sabres', stressing that although the idea of a light sabre is science fiction, the concept of light being used to cut, mend and stick is a scientific reality. Read the other uses of lasers on photocopiable page 35, highlighting how common their use has become over the last 20 years. Use the bar codes on the children's reading books and the use of laser printers to illustrate their wide usage and encourage the children to find and research further examples of lasers of their own.

Page 36: Bar code bonanza!
Learning objective
To consider a range of sources of information to answer questions.

This activity is a useful extension to photocopiable page 35, focusing on the use of bar codes that are 'read' by lasers. Ask the children to collect bar codes from different items (food labels and magazines

being the most disposable). Ask them to take a look at the collection in pairs and write down any observations. Encourage the children to look for holograms, too, and use the internet to find out how lasers are used in their creation.

Page 37: Testing the scientist!
Learning objective
To understand that light travels.
To consider a range of sources of information to answer questions.
To think about what might happen, deciding what evidence to collect.

Start this session with a short example of how to take a vote to gauge opinion (for example, 'School dinners are actually very nutritious and totally delicious: agree or disagree?') Apply this principle to science and ask the children to vote on the motion that light travels in a straight line through air. Use the activity on photocopiable page 37 to stress the value of fair testing and checking answers. Take another class vote afterwards and encourage the children to talk through their discovery process, using the words 'prove' and 'disprove'.

Pages 38, 39 & 40: A dog's diary 1, 2 & 3
Learning objective
To understand that light travels.
To think about what might happen, deciding what evidence to collect.

Recap any work that you may have done about forces and the work of Sir Isaac Newton. Use the story on photocopiables 38 and 39 to introduce the concept that light can be 'cut' up and looked at, and that light is made up of different colours. Read the story as a whole class and then show your class a prism. Ask what they see when they shine a light through it, encouraging them to record this in colour on photocopiable page 40. They should see a full rainbow spectrum. Now introduce the concept of a thought experiment – an experiment that scientists imagine in their heads. Ask the children to imagine what would happen if only the red light passed through the slit in the card and explain what would happen to the light from the second prism. In fact they should still only see the red light since the light now only contains this colour. Give prizes for the wittiest as well as the most scientifically correct ideas for what should go in Sir Isaac's speech bubble!

PART 4:
EXTENSION, ASSESSMENT AND QUIZ

Pages 41, 42 & 43: The adventures of Super-Photon!
Learning objective
To think creatively in science.
To use a wide range of methods to communicate data.

This activity can be used as an extension to your work on light for high-achieving groups or as a whole-class project. Use photocopiable page 41 to introduce the concept of atoms being so small that we cannot see them and that photons are smaller still. Explain that light is made up of millions of photons. Read the adventures of Super-Photon together as a class and decide what makes it a good story. Ask the children what they learned from the comic strip and how this style of storytelling can help us learn 'difficult' things more easily. Explain to the children that they are going to have the chance to bring 'Super-Photon' to life in an action drama. Use photocopiable page 42 to help focus ideas and thoughts for the drama piece. Stress to the children that action involves movement and encourage choreography in order to tell the tale. Try to avoid having your class just standing holding scripts too much as this can inhibit creativity and naturalness. Use photocopiable page 42 to extend and formalise ideas, and photocopiable page 43 for a poster to promote the performance.

Pages 44, 45, 46 & 47: Professor Buzzoff's great experiment-a-thon! 1, 2, 3 & 4
Learning objective
To assess children's knowledge of light.

The activities on these photocopiable pages are all small-scale practical investigations into light and can be used as an assessment at the end of your scheme of work or as reinforcement along the way. The experiment-a-thon can be completed carousel style in an afternoon or spread over several shorter sessions. Set up the five activities and split your class into five working groups. Give each group a copy of the instructions on photocopiable pages 44, 45 and 46, and give each individual a copy of photocopiable page 47 to record their thoughts and discoveries. The experiments on photocopiable page 44 require a dark room, while those on page 45 wotk best in a light room. The 'ghost of a chance' experiment on page 46 will require more time than the others. The aim of this session is to encourage scientific investigation so once it has been completed bring the teams together to discuss their findings. Use the discovery sheet as the basis to decide what makes a 'good' experiment and to encourage the children to consider these factors to design their own experiments (this has become a popular question in SATs examinations at Year 6).

Page 48: Frightening light quiz!
Learning objective
To assess children's knowledge of light.

Use this quiz as the starting point for your own class quiz. Split your class into research teams, using their recent science work as the basis for their questions. Encourage the children to write a mixture of two-point and three-point questions. Also include a practical round where each group has designed an experiment. The other teams will follow instructions and will decide if the experiment gives a true result or not. Reward teams for research, skills and effort, as well as for the knowledge points accumulated in the quiz itself.

NAME _____   DATE _____

GRUESOME GLOOM

It's easy to make light appear and disappear, isn't it? Every morning light appears in the sky and you don't even have to get out of bed to make it happen. So maybe that's why people take light for granted. And think it's no big deal.

Well, it is.

Imagine the sun doesn't rise tomorrow. Then imagine that all the light bulbs in the world go *phfutt* at the same instant.

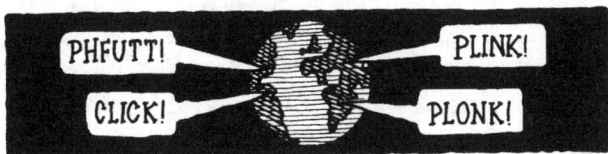

PHFUTT! PLINK! CLICK! PLONK!

And imagine also that even the distant stars fail to shine. The world would be very cold and very dark. And frightening and dangerous. Without light to see by, people would be bumping into each other and treading on the cat and knocking over priceless ornaments and skidding on banana skins.

ARGH! CRASH! MEIOW! SMASH! WHOOPS! SKID!

And that's not all. Can you work out which other things you need light for?

● Make a list of things that we use that rely on light.

1. _____
2. _____
3. _____
4. _____
5. _____
6. _____
8. _____
9. _____
10. _____

● Plan a gruesomely gloomy tale entitled 'THE DAY THE LIGHTS WENT OUT'. Use this story planner to help you.

My Plan

Start: Establish your main **characters** and the **setting**. Use speech to bring your characters to life.
Problem: The lights go out! What is the **effect** of this event? Use your list to help you.
Reaction: How do your characters **react**? How does this affect the setting?
Outcome: It's your story so you can decide what would happen if the lights never came back or if they came back suddenly.
End: What happened to your characters afterwards?

● Now write your gloomy tale!

SEEING THE LIGHT

The sun was sinking behind the Brocken Mountain. The sky was getting darker by the minute and already the climber could scarcely see the narrow twisting goat-path at his feet. The climber was beginning to feel very afraid.

'It's time,' he thought. 'I'm going to see it any minute.' And he peered anxiously at his pocket watch.

'Pull yourself together!' he said to himself. 'You're a scientist. There must be a rational explanation. There's no such thing as ghosts.'

But he trembled and his mouth felt dry as he wondered for the first time how he would find his way down in the dark. A bead of cold sweat trickled down his neck.

Suddenly his heart started thudding. Tiny hairs prickled on the back of his neck.

Somehow he knew even without a backward glance that he was not alone. There was someone … or something on the mountain behind him. He tried to turn his head but his neck had locked rigid. At last

he forced his whole body to swing round. His jaw dropped open in horror. Behind him, etched on the dimming clouds was a huge dark figure. Light played around its ghostly outline as it hung in the air.

The thing seemed to be watching him. Waiting. Waiting to pounce.

For a moment the climber seemed hypnotised. Then he forced himself to react. With trembling hands he pulled out a pocket book and a chewed stub of pencil. And started scribbling unreadable notes. All the time he was mumbling desperately.

'Fascinating phenomenon,' he said, over and over again.

'Fascinating. I – er – better get moving.'

As the climber turned and scurried up the path the giant figure seemed to spring into life. It began climbing silently and effortlessly in the climber's footsteps. And whatever it was, it was coming after him, silently – faster and faster. And reaching out its long shadowy arms…

● What is your theory? Talk about it with your detective group.

NAME _____   DATE _____

Lovely light sources

- Candles are just one source of light.

- What others are there? Look around your classroom and at home.

- Draw these light sources at work in the box below.

The fuel facts

For thousands of years the only fuel for most people was wood to burn in fires. Open fires provided light and heat to roast a juicy hunk of dead mammoth. But around 3000 BC an Egyptian invented the candle. No one knows this person's name but it was a *flaming* good idea – here's how it worked.

5 The gas burns.

6 Flame gives off light and heat energy.

4 Further heat energy turns the wax to gas.

7 Burnt moth supplies extra heat energy.

3 Melted wax is drawn up the wick.

2 Heat energy from the flame melts the wax.

1 The wax (the first candles used solid animal fat) stores energy.

FLAMIN' HECK!

21st-century light!

- But how did we get from our first attempts at harnessing light to the many different choices we have today? Use books and the internet to draw a Terrific Time Line telling the story of humans and how they have used light down the ages.

- Bonus investigation: How can light help you *hear* your favourite CD?

NAME _____   DATE _____

Sunny day at Stonehenge

● Our main source of light is the one that we take most for granted ... the sun!

● But how can the sun help us tell the time?

● You will need:
A stick
Compass
Playground
A sunny day

● Measure the shadow and note the direction it is pointing. Where is the sun?

● Draw all this information in the boxes below. Remember to make a note of the time too!

Bet you never knew!
Some people think that Stonehenge and other rings of stone that were built in – surprise, surprise – the Stone Age are rather large clocks. They lined up with the rising of the sun at special times like Midsummer Day and told the people who built them what day it was. Well, at least they didn't need batteries.

IT'S CALLED A WRISTWATCH

Time:	Time:	Time:	Time:
Length of shadow:	Length of shadow:	Length of shadow:	Length of shadow:
Direction:	Direction:	Direction:	Direction:

● What did you notice?

_____

_____

● How could this help you to tell the time?

_____

_____

NAME _____   DATE _____

A DARING DISCOVERY

Dare you discover ... what light can do?

To begin with:
Wrap some kitchen foil round the end of a small bright torch.

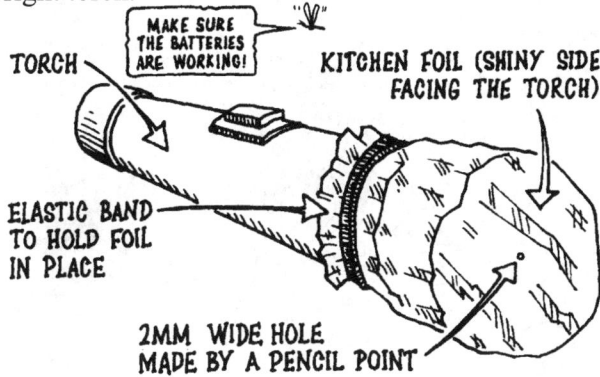

MAKE SURE THE BATTERIES ARE WORKING!

TORCH

KITCHEN FOIL (SHINY SIDE FACING THE TORCH)

ELASTIC BAND TO HOLD FOIL IN PLACE

2MM WIDE HOLE MADE BY A PENCIL POINT

What you need:

ERK! IT'S MILKY AND MURKY!

YOUR TORCH PREPARED AS SHOWN

A SQUARE BOTTLE OR STORAGE JAR WITH 9CM OF WATER. ADD A DROP OF MILK IN WITH THE WATER AND STIR. THE WATER SHOULD BE VERY SLIGHTLY CLOUDY, BUT STILL SEE-THROUGH.

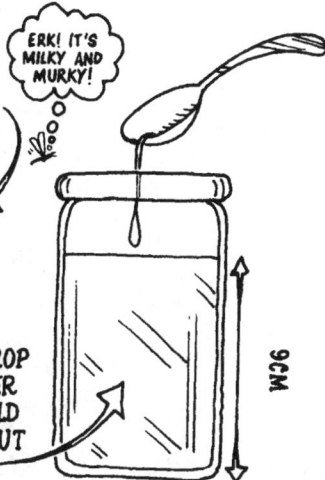

9CM

Experiment 1:
1 Place the jar in front of a dark object. A dark book or some gloomy wallpaper will do.
2 Put your torch up the sides of the jar and switch on the light. You should be able to see the beam of light.
3 Now shine the light up so it hits the underside of the water.

What do you notice?
a) The light seems to flicker like a dodgy television.
b) The light dances sideways.
c) The light seems to bounce down at an angle.

Experiment 2:
Now place the torch about 5cm away from the sides of the jar. Try shining the light up or down from different angles.

What do you notice?
a) From some angles the light beam suddenly jumps to one side as it passes through the sides of the jar.
b) The water begins to heat up and bubble as you move the light.
c) No matter how you move the torch the light beam is always a straight line.

● What did you notice? Write why you think this happens.

● How did you make this a fair test?

_____

_____

_____

_____

NAME _____   DATE _____

The eyes have it!

- We are able to see when light enters our eyes. It's a tricky process ... can you sort it out?

- Match the label numbers to the correct eyeball bits and pieces and write in the table below.

Eyeball bits and pieces		
	label number	relevant fact
Iris		
Eyelashes		
Eye muscles		
Cornea		
Watery bit		
Retina with rod and cone cells*		
Lens		
Ciliary muscles		
Optic nerve		
Sclera (sk-leer-a)		

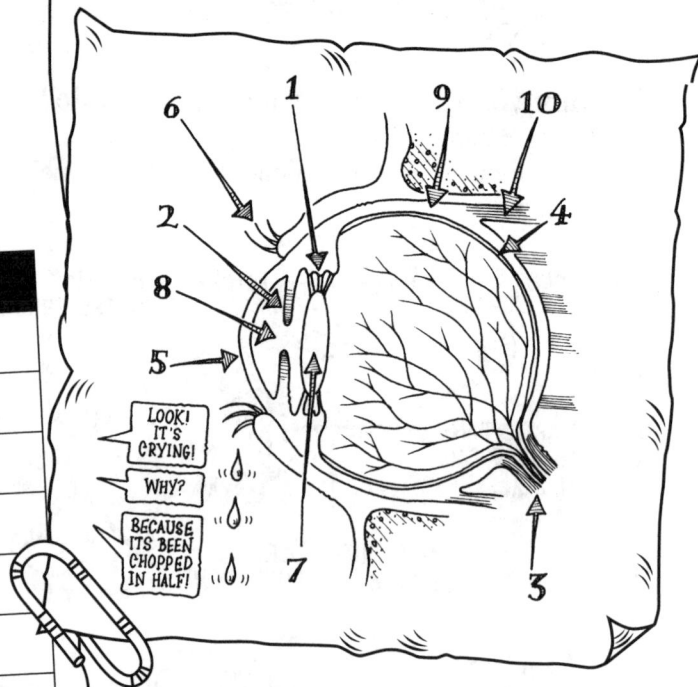

LOOK! IT'S CRYING!

WHY?

BECAUSE ITS BEEN CHOPPED IN HALF!

*By the way the 'cells' are the 60 trillion tiny living jelly-like blobs that make up your body. But you probably knew that already.

- But what do these things actually do? Match these facts to the correct labels in the table above.

Relevant facts
  a) There are 200 of these.
  b) This bit helps to keep the eyeball in shape.
  c) They stop your eyeball slopping out of its socket.
  d) The colour of this bit stops light getting through and dazzling you.
  e) This bit is 6.5 square cm. Without it you'd see nothing.
  f) This bit changes shape 100,000 times a day.
  g) This bit controls the eyeball part mentioned in **f)**.
  h) This part sucks in oxygen gas from the air.
  i) There are one million fibres in this bit.
  j) You can see the blood vessels in this bit.

Bet you never knew?
So how good are your eyeballs? Are they sharp as needles or a sight for sore eyes? Why not put them through their paces? Your eyeballs should be good enough to spot a coin in the playground at 65m. Better make sure the playground is empty before trying this experiment, though.

- Try the coin experiment above in pairs to find out how far you can see.

NAME _____   DATE _____

A handy illusion

Dare you discover ... how something horrible appears to happen to your hand?

What you need:
One red piece of A4 paper
One left hand (Go on, use your own, it won't hurt ... honest!)

What you do:
1 Roll the paper lengthways into a tube 2.5cm across.
2 Stand with a window on your right.
3 Put the tube to your right eye. Stare hard with both eyes open.
4 Place your left hand against the left side of the tube with your thumb underneath the tube.

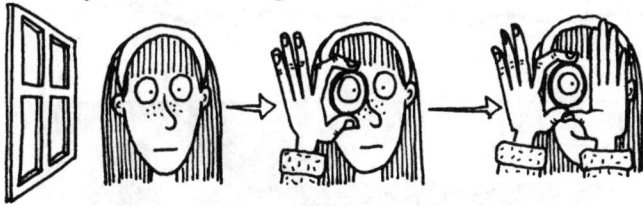

What do you notice?
a) Your hand ... has disappeared.
b) Agggh! A bleeding hole has appeared in your hand.
c) Oh no! You've got two left hands.

● Write up your results and ideas and compare them with your friends.

_____

_____

_____

_____

_____

● Draw your eyeball reflection here. What does the shape remind you of?

Bet you never knew!
Your pupils widen to let in more light in dark conditions. The word 'pupil' comes from the Latin word for 'little girl'. Look at your reflection in a mirror and you'll see a tiny reflection of yourself in your pupil. Sorry boys, the ancient Romans thought this looked like a little girl.

CHEEK!

The awesome eclipse show! 1

One dramatic effect of the sun is called an eclipse. This is caused by the moon getting in the way of the sun's light so that its shadows fall on the earth.

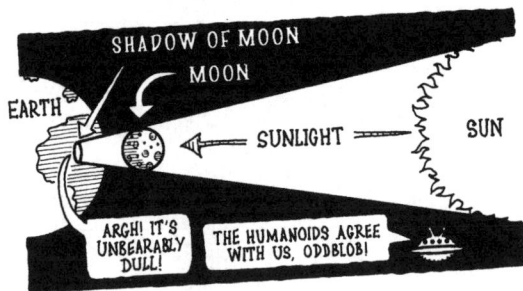

Oh, so you knew that? Well, in the past many people didn't – so they made up stories and performed rituals to make sense of what was going on.

1. An eclipse can be frightening. If you don't know what's happening, it looks like the moon is swallowing the sun. According to ancient Greek writer Thucydides (460–400 BC) an eclipse halted a battle in Persia in the sixth century BC. The two armies drew back and agreed to go on with the battle after a month, when any bad magical effects had worn off.

2. In ancient China people thought a dragon was eating the sun and banged gongs or pans to scare the monster away.

3. The native peoples of North America fired flaming arrows at the sky in a bid to re-light the sun.

4. The Pampas tribes of South America believed the moon goddess was darkened in an eclipse with her own blood drawn by savage dogs. Of course, they were barking up the wrong tree.

5. Some Tartar tribes in Asia believed the sun and moon were swallowed up by a blood-sucking vampire from a distant star.

6. In many countries people thought (wrongly) that diseases spread during eclipses. The Yukon tribes of Alaska covered their pots and pans during eclipses for this reason. A terrible outbreak of 'flu that claimed thousands of victims in South America in 1918 was blamed by some on an eclipse.

The awesome eclipse show! 2

● The cartoon below has been adapted into a play script...

Scene 1: On a space ship

Slobslime: Ahh, there's nothing I like better than just rocketing about the solar system on a sunny Sunday afternoon. Fancy a game of slimeball? (*Slobslime gets a huge ball of green slime and starts counting headers very slowly.*) 1... 2... 3... Er – what's next?

Odd-blob: Hey! You'll mess up the control panel... you know what happened last time! Anyway, I'm planet spotting... There's the moon (*points to a grey planet*) the sun (*points to an orange planet*) and... oh I've forgotten what that one's called... It's got those dim-witted humanoids living all over it... I'll take a closer look at it through the spacecraft sensor screen...

Slobslime: I don't know why you bother looking at planets. It's not like anything ever changes out there – ooops! (*squelching sound*)

Scene 2: Meanwhile at Sunny Town beach...

Jenny: (*Carrying a loud CD player and lots of beach stuff.*) Hurry up, Gran! There's not much space left!

Gran: Sorry dear, I'm coming as fast as I can. Now where did I put that knitting? (*Rummages in her bag and brings out a really gross jumper.*)

Jenny: Glad you found it – not! Look, there's Kadir and Lois, they saved us a spot.

Kadir: Hi Jenny, you just made it in time. There's a sandcastle-building contest today and we've made a start. First prize is a bunch of computer games and as much ice cream you can eat without being sick!

Jenny: Wow!

Gran: Now, before you start to get involved in that sort of thing you all need your sun cream. It's no use pulling faces, Jenny, it's for your own good and the sun is so strong today that you certainly need protection. You first, Lois...

Scene 3: Back on the space ship
(*Odd-blob is trying to clean up the control panel with blurbi-spray.*)

Odd-blob: I told you not to play slime ball in here but you wouldn't take a teensy bit of notice and now look what's happened! And stay away from things you might break! (*Slobslime is staring at the sensor screen. Suddenly she looks scared.*)

Slobslime: Odd-blob! Come here...

Odd-blob: Shhh, can't you see I'm busy cleaning up your mess?

(*The sun, the moon and Earth begin to move into an eclipse position.*)

Slobslime: Odd-blob, I mean it, your planet thingies, they're um... scaring me...

Odd-blob: Don't be silly, you said yourself that they never change! Anyway, we'll be late and you'll miss your slimeburgers!

● How would an eclipse affect Jenny's day at the seaside? What would it look like from space for the aliens? Complete the script using the characters and dialogue and add any stage directions that might be useful.

NAME _____   DATE _____

The awesome eclipse show! 3

Dark secrets

It gets dark during an eclipse because the moon casts its shadow over the Earth. You get a shadow any time a solid object blocks light. (That's how the climber on the Brocken Mountain made the 'ghost'.) Something that blocks light is described as opaque (o-payk). And you can use an opaque shape to make horrible shadows...

Dare you discover ... what lurks in the shadows?

What you need:
A pencil
A pair of scissors
A piece of black card. You can always paint a white piece of card black.
A piece of wire
Sticky tape
A small, bright torch
A room with light walls.

What you do:
1. Draw and cut out a monster shape.
2. Tape the wire to the bottom of the shape to make a handle.
3. Wait until it gets dark. Draw the curtains and switch on your torch. Place the torch about three metres from the wall.

4. Hold the wire so the shape is between the light and the wall. You can make brilliant sinister shadows. Hold on, sorry to spoil things, but this is a serious scientific experiment, after all. So...

What do you notice?
a) You moved the shape towards the wall and away from the torch. The shadow on the wall got larger.
b) When the shape is closer to the light it blocks more light. This throws a larger shadow on the wall.
c) As you moved the torch the shadow began to move in the opposite direction. Help – it's alive!

● What happened? Write your answer and include your reasons why.

_____

_____

_____

● Now use your awesome eclipse scripts to perform a shadow-theatre play for your class. Design shadow puppets to act out your play and include as many lighting effects as you can!

- Use books and the internet to research more creatures that glow in the dark and add them to the zoo.

- Try and find out how they manage to glow!

- What non-living things do you know that also glow in the dark? Draw a glow-in-the-dark gallery and label your exhibits.

Could you be a scientist?

It's 200 years ago. You're walking home and you bravely decide to take a short cut through the graveyard. It's very dark – you're scared ... and suddenly you see an eerie glow. What's causing it?

a) It's a ghost. Yikes, I'm out of here.

b) It's a mass of glow-worms feeding off rotting vegetation.

c) It's gases from a rotting body.

The glow-in-the-dark zoo!

THE GLOW IN THE DARK ZOO

Welcome to the world's first zoo where the animals provide the lighting ...

Comb Jelly
Jelly-fish-like creature 25–30cm (9.8–11.8 inches) long.

FOUND IN: Pacific and Atlantic Oceans.

LIGHT IS USED FOR: scaring off attackers.

LIGHT-PRODUCING CELLS ON RIDGES ALL ALONG ITS BODY

'COMB' HERE

NO FEAR!

Deep sea angler fish
FOUND IN: deep oceans throughout the world

LIGHT IS USED FOR: catching other fish

WORM-LIKE BLOB (FILLED WITH GLOWING BACTERIA) ON THE END OF A LINE LURES SMALLER FISH TO THEIR DOOM.

HMMM, INTERESTING!

Fire flies and glow-worms

FOUND IN: fire flies live in North America and glow-worms live in Europe. Actually they're both varieties of beetle.

LIGHT IS USED FOR: signalling for a mate.

PHWOAR! HE'S NICE!

FIRE FLY

HERE I AM, BOYS!

GLOW-WORM

Both insects have glowing lights on their bottoms. (Imagine you had one of these – you'd never need a rear bike light.)

Luminous plankton

Tiny creatures often less than 1 mm (0.04 inches) long called copepods (cope-pods). The plankton also include plants called dinoflagellates (di-no-fladge-gell-ates).

FOUND IN: every ocean especially where the water is rich in minerals.

LIGHT IS USED FOR: scaring away attackers. Ship toilets are often flushed with seawater – if the plankton are present they make your toilet glow in the dark. (Is this what they call a "flash in the pan"?)

COPEPOD

DINOFLAGELLATE

ARGH! WEIRD WEE WEE!

AWFUL ADVERTISING

Ye olde LIGHT UP YOUR LIFE — Home shopping catalogue

NOW WE HAVE TO WAIT 3500 YEARS FOR SOMEONE TO INVENT MATCHES

ROMANTIC CANDLES Why not light your home with a genuine olde worlde candle as used by people since ancient Egyptian times. Wow, what a dazzling choice!

- The Light Up Your Life catalogue is about to launch its own home-shopping television network!
- Use these adverts to research different light sources. Add some other light sources of your own.
- Design your own television adverts to persuade viewers to buy your product instead of someone else's!

Traditional tallow candle
▷ Made with boiled-up fat from around the kidneys of a dead cow, sheep or horse.

THE SMALL PRINT: Tallow candles are smelly and greasy. They go out easily and the pong is so bad that in parts of the West Indies the candles are lit to keep the bugs at bay.

WE'VE RUN OUT OF TALLOW CANDLES, WIFE

Heat from the flame melts the fat

▷ Beeswax – the de-luxe alternative. Genuine waxy stuff squirted from the bodies of bees and built up to make chambers for their grubs to live in.

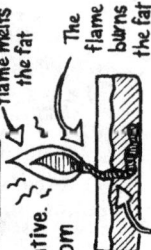

The flame burns the fat

The wick sucks up the fat

Modern paraffin candle
▷ Made from oil.
▷ Burns with a nice bright flame

THE SMALL PRINT: It's still a fire hazard and melted wax can drip everywhere and make a mess. Oh, and the light can become dim and flickering if you don't trim the wick.

SORRY, MUM, IT'S MADE A MESS...
GRRR, I'LL GIVE YOU WAX!

THE AMAZING ARC-LIGHT
Invented by British scientist Sir Humphrey Davy (1778-1829) in 1808
▷ Electric current jumps across the gap between two carbon rods. (Make sure there's a constant gap between

WELL, CANDLES WENT OUT WITH THE ARK

two carbon rods as the light burns otherwise the rods will melt or the light will fizzle out.)

THE SMALL PRINT: This light is a fire hazard. And it could blind you because it's brighter than 4,000 candles. The only practical use anyone ever found for it was in the Dungeness lighthouse. So unless your house happens to be a lighthouse it's probably not such a good idea.

TURN IT OFF!
Electric current
Glowing carbon rod

GASLIGHT
As invented by Scottish inventor William Murdock (1754-1839) after an experiment in 1792 involving heating coal in his mum's teapot.

Flame made by burning coal gas

Handy tap to turn the gas on or off

ER – I'M JUST WARMING THE POT, MUM.
GRRR!

THE SMALL PRINT: You need pipes all over your house to carry the gas. And the gas is poisonous and can blow up your home. And even when it works the flame is smoky and smelly.

MARVELLOUS MODERN LIGHTS
Nowadays things are looking much brighter. Go into any street and you'll probably see sodium or mercury street lights. These work in roughly the same way.

An electric current passes through the tube. Atoms in the gas take in energy and give out light.

Something else passing through a tube

NAME _____ DATE _____

BRIGHTER BULBS

FILAMENT

THE ARGON GAS ACTS AS A BUILT IN FIRE EXTINGUISHER

ARGH! I'M 'ARGON'ER

FLUTTER

- Draw your light bulb in the box below.

- Label the different parts, explaining what job they do to help the bulb work. (Use books and the internet to find out the facts.)

My bulb

Bet you never knew!
Light bulbs save lives. Nowadays many lighthouses use electric light from powerful bulbs to warn ships away from rocks. Each lighthouse has its own pattern of flashes so that sailors can work out where they are in the dark.

ER, HANG ON ...TWO LONG FLASHES, ONE SHORT ONE...

CRUNCH!

- We use light bulbs in lots of different places.

- Research some of the uses and describe the differences in the type of bulbs that are used. Explain why we don't use the same type of bulb for each job.

NAME _____   DATE _____

Miraculous mirrors 1

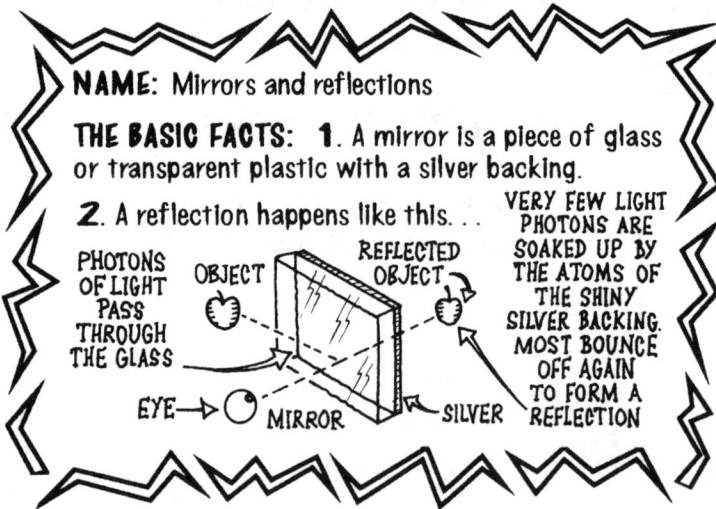

NAME: Mirrors and reflections

THE BASIC FACTS: **1.** A mirror is a piece of glass or transparent plastic with a silver backing.

2. A reflection happens like this...

PHOTONS OF LIGHT PASS THROUGH THE GLASS

OBJECT

REFLECTED OBJECT

VERY FEW LIGHT PHOTONS ARE SOAKED UP BY THE ATOMS OF THE SHINY SILVER BACKING. MOST BOUNCE OFF AGAIN TO FORM A REFLECTION

EYE → ○   MIRROR   SILVER

Spot the reflection quiz

Reflections can help...

1 Road signs glow in the dark. TRUE/FALSE
2 Clouds glow in the sky. TRUE/FALSE
3 A television set show pictures. TRUE/FALSE
4 A shellfish see. TRUE/FALSE

I'M NOT TELLING YOU!

I CAN'T WINKLE IT OUT OF HIM

5 A doctor peer inside your eyeball. TRUE/FALSE
6 A mirage appear. TRUE/FALSE
7 Astronomers detect a black hole in space. TRUE/FALSE
8 The snow blind you. TRUE/FALSE

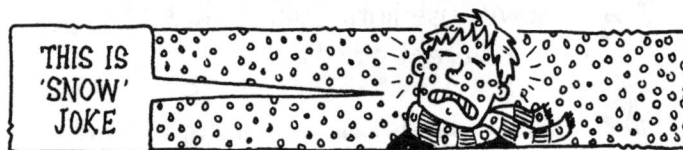

THIS IS 'SNOW' JOKE

9 A surgeon peer inside your body without cutting you open. TRUE/FALSE

Answers:

1 TRUE. You can find tiny mirrors in road signs and in road studs. The mirrors reflect car headlights. **2 TRUE.** Clouds reflect sunlight. That's what makes them bright and glowing. Thunderclouds appear dark and gloomy from the ground because they are thicker than ordinary clouds and reflect most of the sunlight upwards. Clouds that glow at night do so because they are high enough in the sky to still catch the sunlight. **3 FALSE.** There are no mirrors inside a television set. **4 TRUE.** Scallops are a type of shellfish with tiny mirrors in their eyes. Each eye has a shiny layer of crystals that reflect light on to cells inside the eye. A scientist made this discovery while looking down a microscope at the shellfish. He saw his own face reflected in the creature's 100 gruesome eyes. **5 TRUE.** A doctor uses an ophthalmoscope (op-thal-mo-scope) to peer inside your eyeball. This instrument shines a light on to a curved mirror that focuses the light beam into your eyeball. The doctor then peers through a hole in the middle of the mirror to inspect your nerves and blood vessels. **6 FALSE.** Mirages are caused by refraction. (Just to remind you, refraction is bended light.) **7 FALSE.** Light can't escape from a black hole (that's why they're black). So you can't spot one with a mirror. **8 TRUE.** Snow reflects light so well that you can be blinded by staring at it for too long in bright sunlight. That's why skiers wear protective goggles. **9 TRUE.** The tube is called an endoscope and it's basically two bundles of optical fibres. One bundle takes light from a light source at one end into the body – just imagine sticking a torch down your throat. The surgeon looks through the other bundle to get a close-up of your innards.

● Now research your own miraculous mirror questions...

NAME _____ DATE _____

Miraculous mirrors 2

Dare you discover ... what a mirror does to light?
What you need:
A mirror
Two eyebrows and yourself

What you do:
1 Stand in front of the mirror.
2 Raise your left eyebrow. (If you can't do this just point to your left eyebrow instead.)

What does your reflection do?
a) It raises its left eyebrow.
b) The reflection raises its right eyebrow.
c) The reflection raises its right eyebrow but there's a delay of about half a second.

Answer: b) That's because the light arriving from the right of a mirror always reflects to the left at the same angle. And you got it – the light from the right leaves to the left. This means that you see the image in the mirror the wrong way round.

LIGHT ARRIVING FROM THE LEFT REFLECTS TO THE RIGHT

LIGHT ARRIVING FROM THE RIGHT REFLECTS TO THE LEFT

● What do you think will happen? Explain why.

_____

● Try out the experiment. What actually happened?

_____
_____

● To test out your theory, use a mirror on the answer box above!

● Try the theory out for yourself! Write a secret mirror message to your mates.

My Mirror Message

My Mirror Message

● Try drawings too!

NAME _____ DATE _____

Murderous mirrors!

• Early people realised that shiny surfaces were great for seeing yourself in. Very handy for helping you brush your hair properly or spot an embarrassing bogie in your nostril.

ARGH!

• In ancient Egypt all sorts of things were used as mirrors including polished metal, wet slates and bowls of water. But none of them was smooth enough to give a clear, bright image. (In order to see your reflection you need a smooth surface so the photons reflect back together – remember?)

BRIGHT, AREN'T WE?

• By the time the Romans came along mirrors were much improved. The Romans used glass to make mirrors with a thin backing of tin. Unfortunately, this invention was to cause a few heated moments. According to legend the Greek scientist Archimedes (287–212 BC) used a bank of mirrors to burn Roman ships that were attacking his home city.

Every mirror reflected sunlight on to a single point on the ship. The wood heated up and burst into flames. This is scientifically possible although there's no proof it happened.

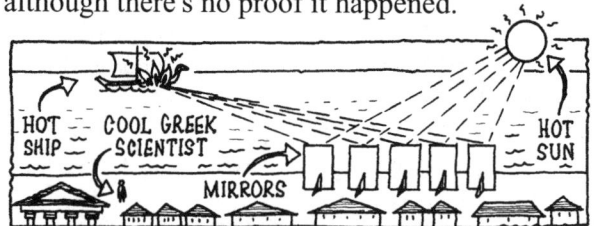

HOT SHIP   COOL GREEK SCIENTIST   MIRRORS   HOT SUN

• In the Middle Ages Venice made the finest mirrors in the world. Venetians had learnt to use a mixture of mercury and tin for the backing which was easy to work without heating. This mixture was top secret. A special island was set aside for this work but the mercury was poisonous and many workers died or were driven mad by it. Nevertheless, they were forbidden to pass on the secret on pain of death.

THIS SECRET IS DEADLY. IT'S DEATH IF WE TALK ABOUT IT AND DEATH IF WE DON'T

● Check out the story about the Greeks and Romans for yourself. Use the diagram to help you recreate the scene. You will need a torch to represent the sun (teachers don't like it if you start a real fire in the classroom!).

● If you can use the mirrors to reflect the sun onto the ships then you will have won the battle! What do you think you might have to do to make this happen?

_____

_____

● Use a protractor to help you measure any important angles. Add this information to an illustrated instruction sheet called 'How to sink a boat with a mirror!'

NAME _____   DATE _____

SURPRISING SPOONS

Dare you discover ... how mirrors can change your appearance?

What you need:
A shiny tablespoon

1 Hold the spoon like a hand mirror.
2 Look in the back of the spoon and then the front.

What do you notice?
a) My face appears upside down in the back of the spoon and the right way up in the front.
b) My face appears fatter in the back of the spoon and upside down with a long neck in the front of the spoon.
c) My face appears normal in the back of the spoon. In the front of the spoon I'm the right way up but I have a huge hooter.

● Draw what you see on the front and the back of the spoon:

● Why do you think this is?

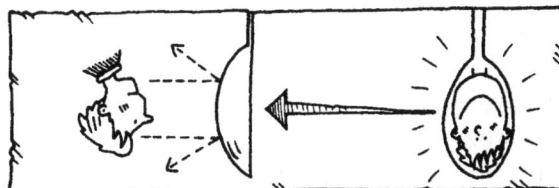

_____

_____

_____

Answer: b) The front of the spoon is concave — that is it curves inwards at the centre. (To remember this word, just imagine a cave shaped in the same way.)

CONCAVE SPOON
CONCAVE CAVE

Because of this shape, light reflecting from your face reflects downwards from the top of the spoon and upwards from the bottom.

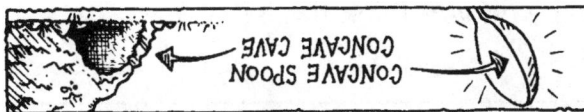

You see the bottom of your face at the top of the spoon and the top at the bottom. And your face appears upside down. Turn the spoon around and you're faced with a bulging or, as scientists say, a convex shape.

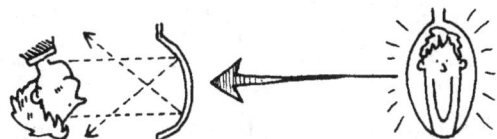

CONVEX MIRROR
BULGING CENTRE
BULGING TUMMY
CONVEX SCIENTIST

The convex shape reflects the light from your face and spreads it slightly outwards. This makes your face appear rounder and fatter (though this time you're the right way up!).

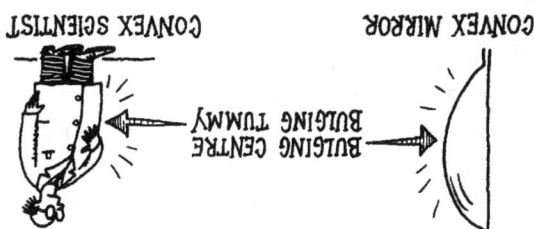

HORRIBLE HEALTH WARNING!

Your parents may not appreciate you performing this interesting experiment at meal times. Especially when the posh relatives are waiting for their brussels sprouts and you're using the best silver tablespoon.

NAME _____   DATE _____

The Mystery of Mirror Mansion

Dare you discover ... how to make a ghost appear?
What you need:
Sticky tape
Scissors
A small but bright torch
A mirror – about 24cm x 36cm is ideal
A piece of black paper (larger than your mirror)
A pencil
A large black water-based felt-tippped marker
A room with light-coloured walls.

What you do:
1 Draw the outline of your ghost on the black paper. This should be smaller than the mirror.
2 Cut out the outline.
3 Stick the remaining paper with the ghost shape removed over the mirror.
4 Use the felt tip to draw in the features of your ghost in the ghost shape on the mirror.

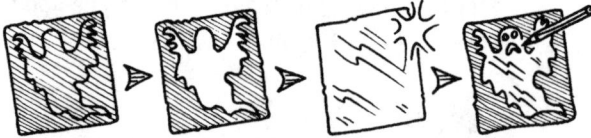

5 Darken the room. Better still wait until nightfall – after all, that's when ghosts appear.

6 Prop the mirror securely on an armchair. The mirror should be facing the wall about two metres away. Shine your torch at the mirror. Your ghost appears on the wall.
7 Move the torch so the ghost appears to float in the air.

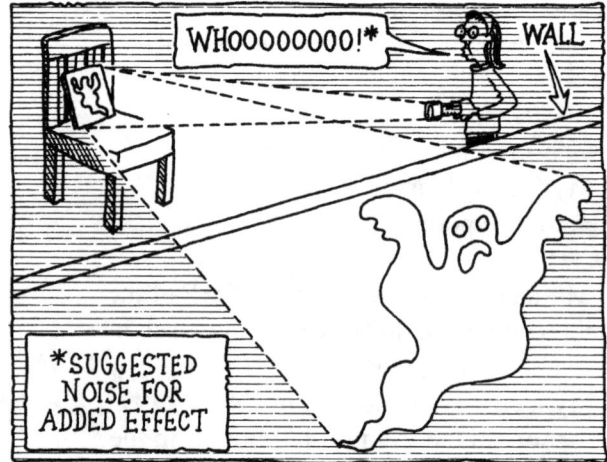

WHOOOOOOOO!* WALL

*SUGGESTED NOISE FOR ADDED EFFECT

What is the scientific explanation for the ghost?
a) The torchlight reflects off the black paper and the felt-tipped lines.
b) The light reflects off the mirror but not the paper or the lines.
c) The light reflects off everything.

● Why do you think this is?

_____

_____

● Now start a story starring your very own ghost ... The Mystery of Mirror Mansion!

> **Setting:** An old creepy house known as 'Mirror Mansion'.
> **Characters:** You, two friends, a sinister butler and a ghost.
> **Start:** You are on a school trip but the coach breaks down in a storm. You volunteer to go and get help with some friends. The storm forces you towards an old house with a single candle burning at the window.

● What will you find? How will you escape? What is the ghost up to? How could a mirror help you? It's all up to you!

NAME _____   DATE _____

Ridiculous refraction 1

What have all these things got in common?

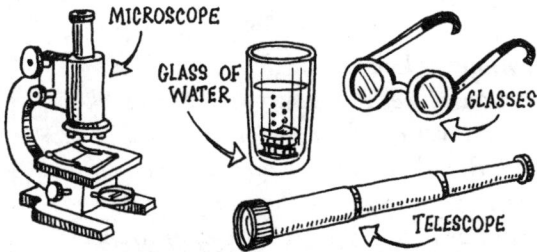

MICROSCOPE

GLASS OF WATER

GLASSES

TELESCOPE

Yes, I know they all contain glass but that *isn't* the only CORRECT answer. Give up? Well, the other answer is that they all bend or refract light. But how do they do it?

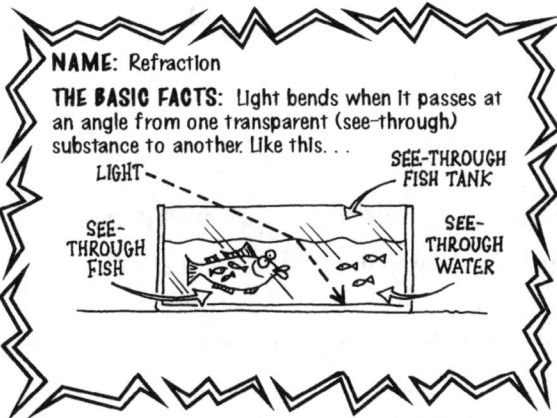

NAME: Refraction

THE BASIC FACTS: Light bends when it passes at an angle from one transparent (see-through) substance to another. Like this. . .

LIGHT

SEE-THROUGH FISH TANK

SEE-THROUGH FISH

SEE-THROUGH WATER

Here's a slow-motion replay of refraction as light hits that fish tank…

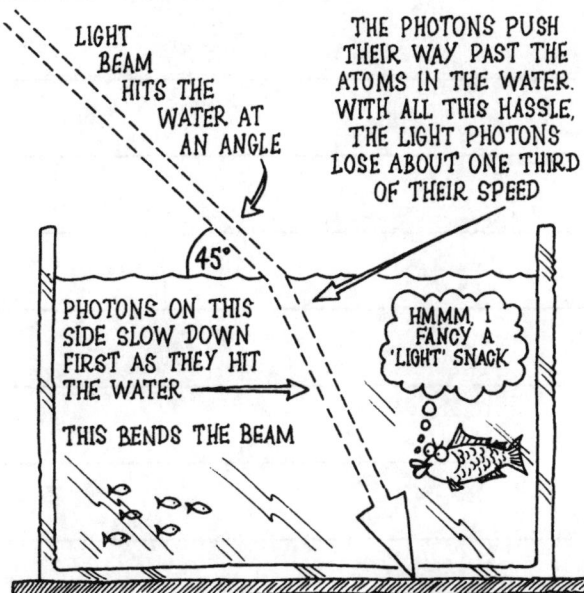

LIGHT BEAM HITS THE WATER AT AN ANGLE

THE PHOTONS PUSH THEIR WAY PAST THE ATOMS IN THE WATER. WITH ALL THIS HASSLE, THE LIGHT PHOTONS LOSE ABOUT ONE THIRD OF THEIR SPEED

45°

PHOTONS ON THIS SIDE SLOW DOWN FIRST AS THEY HIT THE WATER

THIS BENDS THE BEAM

HMMM, I FANCY A 'LIGHT' SNACK

- Try it for yourself! Draw what your tank looks like with the objects in it but without the water.

- Then draw it after the water is added.

Without water

With water

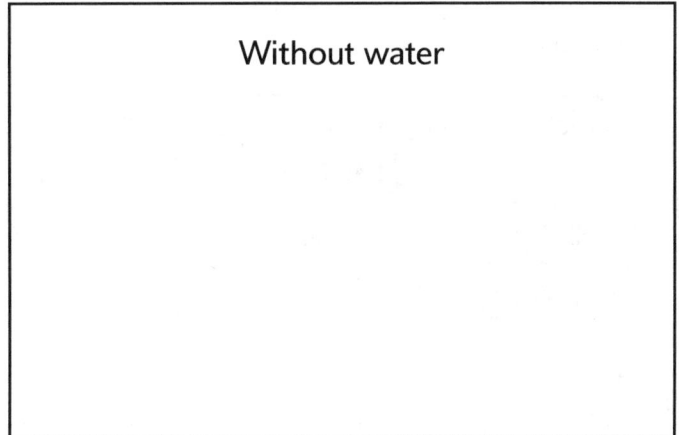

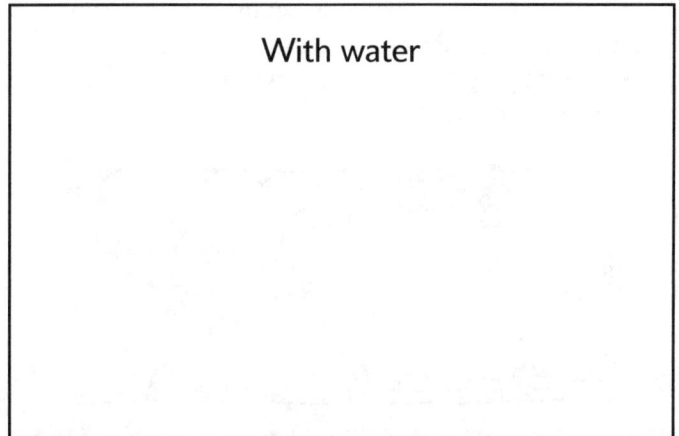

- What differences do you notice? How can you create the illusion of having six objects?

_____
_____
_____
_____
_____

NAME _____ DATE _____

Ridiculous refraction 2

Dare you discover ... how to make a coin disappear?

What you need:

A £1 coin

A washbasin

A ruler

OK, AS LONG AS IT DOESN'T DISAPPEAR DOWN THE SWEETSHOP

What you do:

1 Fill the basin with water to a depth of 4cm.

2 Place the coin in the water.

3 Crouch down so that you can just see the coin over the rim of the washbasin.

4 Lift the plug slightly so the water level in the sink falls slowly.

NO "CHANGE" YET, DAD

As the water drains down the plughole the coin gradually disappears. *Why?*

a) Grrrr! My coin has gone down the drain!

b) The water refracted the light reflecting back from the coin so it made the coin look further away than it really was.

c) The light from the coin was refracted so the coin appeared closer.

Bet you never knew!

Refraction causes mirages. In hot places like deserts a layer of warm air forms over the ground. But above this the air can be much colder. Light from the sky speeds up and bends sideways as it passes from the cooler to the hotter air. As a result, light from the sky shines along the ground. And thirsty travellers see this light as a watery-looking blue on the horizon.

WATER LOVELY SIGHT!

● Why do you think this happens? Write your theory and discuss it with your group.

_____

_____

_____

_____

_____

_____

_____

_____

_____

_____

_____

_____

NAME _____ DATE _____

CRUCIAL COLOURS

The colourful facts

A green leaf or caterpillar soaks up all the colours in light except green. Green reflects off the leaf (or caterpillar) and that's what you see.

GARDENER'S GREEN FINGERS

GREEN PLANT

GREEN CATERPILLAR

A ripe tomato soaks up all kinds of light except red.

YOU'RE AN AMAZING GARDENER!

RED BLUSH!

White objects reflect every kind of light. (Don't forget white light is all the colours mixed up.)

POLAR BEAR IN THE SNOW (WEARING A WHITE BOBBLE HAT).

Dare you discover ... where colour comes from?

What you need:
A nice juicy red tomato
A piece of white A4 paper
A small but bright torch

What you do:
1 Darken the room or better still wait for nightfall.
2 Place the tomato on one end of the paper.
3 Hold the torch over the paper level with the tomato. Shine the light on the tomato.

WHOSE BRIGHT IDEA WAS THIS?

4 Look at the area of shadow under the torch beam. It should be glowing pink. *Why?*
a) The tomato is reflecting red light on to the paper.
b) It's a trick of my eyes caused by the torchlight.
c) The shadow of the tomato is soaking up all the colours in light except red.

NAME: Colours

THE BASIC FACTS: 1. White light contains all the colours in the rainbow – remember that bit? In fact, each colour is caused by a light wave of a particular size.

2. When light hits an object some of the colours are soaked up and others are reflected. And it's the reflected colours that we see. Got all that?

THE FRIGHTENING DETAILS: When something is black all the colours in light are soaked up so nothing reflects back. This explains the colour of this big black revolting slug.

YEAH, CHEERS!

● Why do you think this happens?

_____

_____

_____

_____

_____

_____

_____

_____

_____

_____

_____

NAME _____   DATE _____

Mysterious mixing

Crucial colour vision

Whatever colours you manage to mix you'll need a pair of eyes to appreciate them. Humans, birds and apes are lucky in this respect. We view the world in glorious living Technicolor. Unlike, for example, a squid, which can only see black and white or your pet cat who sees green and blue but not red. (Scientists aren't quite sure why this is – but when Tiddles finishes off a mouse she sees the blood and gory bits as green.)

ALL OF A SUDDEN...
I DON'T FEEL HUNGRY

How you see in colour

1 Unlike Tiddles you've actually got three types of cone cells in your retina – one each for green, blue and red light. All the colours you see are made from mixing at least two of these colours.

2 Your incredible eyes are able to make out up to ten million different colours. It's amazing to think they can do this from just three basic colours.

Bet you never knew!

Colour photos are made by mixing different light colours.

1 The first colour picture was taken by Scottish physicist James Clerk Maxwell (1831–1879). In 1863 he took three snaps of one of his wife's ribbons. One through a red filter, one blue and one green. Each filter blocked all the colours in light except its particular colour. So the green filter, for example, showed up the green parts of the pattern. He combined the images to make a colour picture.

FASCINATING, CAN I HAVE IT BACK NOW?

2 Nowadays, though, colour films consist of three layers of chemicals. The top layer makes a blue colour from blue light, the second makes green in the same way and the third makes a red colour. Between them the chemicals build up an image. Our brains do the rest of the colour mixing.

● Draw and colour an object as you see it, then imagine seeing it through a cat and a squid's eyes!

What I see	What the cat sees	What the squid sees
My object:		

● What I noticed:

_____

_____

NAME _____   DATE _____

Colour vision!

Dare you discover ... how you see colours?
What you need:
A piece of black paper
A small piece of yellow paper about 3cm square
Your head complete with eyeballs.

What you do:
1 Place the yellow paper on the black paper and stare at it for 30 seconds without moving your head or blinking.

● What do you see? Draw it here and write a short description.

[drawing box]

_____
_____
_____
_____

2 You should see a square of blue appearing round the edge of the yellow square.

OK, so where does it come from?
a) The cells that fire blue signals take time to work – but now they've detected blue colouring in the black paper.
b) The yellow paper has excited your blue cells so much they've gone into overdrive. And now you're seeing too much blue.
c) The green and red cells that give you yellow are getting tired but the blue cells are still firing.

● Which theory would you choose? Give reasons for this.

_____
_____
_____
_____
_____
_____

Test your art teacher
If you mix green and red and blue light together you'll get a pale whitish sort of a colour. But if you mix together green and red and blue paints you get black – why?

Bet you never knew!
Is your street lit by sodium lights? (These are the bright orange lights.) In this light (provided there are no other types of light near by) red things such as lipstick, blood or geraniums appear black. Sodium light contains no red light. Because red objects can't reflect any red light you see them as black.

WE'RE GOING TO A DISCO NOT A FUNERAL

WHY ARE YOU WEARING BLACK LIPSTICK, THEN?

NAME _____   DATE _____

LASER MATHS

● Use the information box to calculate these light-tastic teasers!

1 How long would it take a laser signal to travel around the earth **three** times?

_____

_____

2 How long would it take a laser signal to make a **single** trip to the moon?

_____

_____

3 The moon's distance from Earth varies as it goes around our planet. Assume it's 374,740km from Earth. Use this figure to calculate the speed the light from the laser is travelling.

_____

_____

Speedy signals

Don't forget light is *FAST* with a capital F. And so is laser light.

● In 0.14 seconds you can send a laser signal around the world.

OUCH! I TOLD YOU TO POINT THAT LASER AWAY FROM ME!

I DID BUT IT WENT ROUND THE WORLD AND SHOT YOU IN THE BUM

● In 2.5 seconds you can send a light signal to the moon *and* back again. (In the 1960s US scientists did this. By timing the signal they were able to calculate the exact distance of the moon.)

● A laser could send a light signal to Mars in just three minutes. (The Martians' reply would take another three minutes.)

THIS IS PLANET EARTH. . . IS THERE ANYTHING TO EAT ON YOUR WORLD?

3 MINUTES

YES EARTHLINGS – MARZ BARS, MARZIPAN, AND MARTIAN MALLOWS

● Show your working out here...

WELL, THAT'S BRIGHTENED UP MY DAY!

● Now make up some of your own laser maths questions to try on your friends.

NAME ——————————————— DATE ———————————

LASER HALL OF FAME!

● Lasers can be life-savers. They can cut through human flesh and heat seal the edges of a wound so you don't get bleeding. By firing a laser down an endoscope (that's a tube containing optical fibres) you can perform life-saving operations deep within the body. A laser can even weld back a retina that has come adrift from the inside of the eyeball.

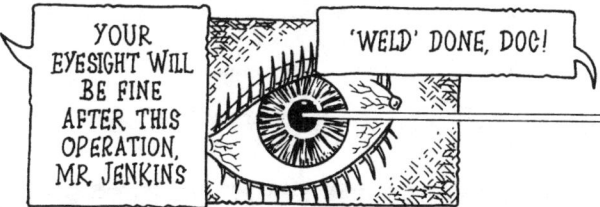

YOUR EYESIGHT WILL BE FINE AFTER THIS OPERATION, MR. JENKINS

'WELD' DONE, DOC!

● A laser beam 'reads' a CD by flickering as it reflects off a pattern of pits on its surface. The CD player turns this flickering light signal into electric pulses and then into your fave pop music.

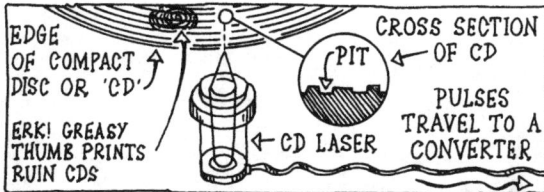

EDGE OF COMPACT DISC OR 'CD'

ERK! GREASY THUMB PRINTS RUIN CDS

CROSS SECTION OF CD
PIT
← CD LASER
PULSES TRAVEL TO A CONVERTER

● Laser beams travel in straight lines so you can use them to build nice straight tunnels. Simply fire a beam from the entrance of the tunnel and get digging along the line of the beam.
● A laser beam can melt and weld metals. And unlike any other tool a laser beam never gets blunt with use.
● Laser beams liven up pop concerts. Simply fire the laser into the air and wave it around to make dramatic light patterns. And then who cares if the music's rubbish?
● Lasers can measure tiny earthquakes. Lasers on the San Andreas Fault, California are linked up to monitoring equipment. Any wobble in the light beam caused by a tremor in the ground can be instantly detected.

SORRY, THAT TREMOR WAS MY FAULT - WE HAD BAKED BEAN STEW FOR TEA LAST NIGHT

● What other ways can we use lasers?

Clues

Take a look at the **back** of your reading book

Think about the different kinds of printers that are available

● Draw and write your findings to add to the Laser Hall of Fame.

NAME _____ DATE _____

Bar code bonanza!

Laser beams read bar codes in shops or libraries. Take a look on the back of this book. Can you see a square with a pattern of lines? The pattern is a unique code for this legendary Light activity book owned by your lucky teacher. If you bought the book you may have seen the shop assistant passing a scanner across the lines. A laser beam in the scanner flickers as it picks up the lines and the flickering beam is read by a computer that recognises the code from the pattern of flickers.

ISBN 0-439-97190-X

9 780439 971904

● But are all bar codes the same?

● Collect your labels and compare them. Stick them in these boxes.

Item 1	Item 2	Item 3

● What I noticed:

_____

_____

_____

_____

● Collect some holograms and compare them to an ordinary postcard picture. What differences do you notice?

_____

_____

_____

_____

Bet you never knew!
You can make holograms with lasers. All you have to do is...

BEAM SPLITTER MIRROR
LENS
LENS
MIRROR HOLOGRAPHIC PLATE

Split a laser beam into two beams using a mirror. Fire one of these at an object. Make sure it then reflects on to a photographic plate. The other beam fires directly at the plate. When seen in daylight these dots form a 3-D pattern. Nowadays holograms appear on credit cards to stop crooks from copying them. So this discovery reflects to your credit!

NAME _____   DATE _____

Testing the scientist!

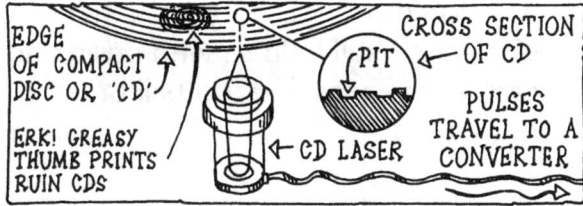

EDGE
OF COMPACT
DISC OR 'CD'

CROSS SECTION
OF CD

PIT ◄── OF CD

PULSES
TRAVEL TO A
CONVERTER

ERK! GREASY
THUMB PRINTS
RUIN CDS

◄─ CD LASER

Laser beams travel in straight lines so you can use them to build nice straight tunnels. Simply fire a beam from the entrance of the tunnel and get digging along the line of the beam.

● Take a look at this statement: Light travels in a straight line through the air.

● Do you agree or disagree? Take a class vote and write your results in the boxes!

agree	disagree

● Use the results from the experiment below to <u>prove</u> or <u>disprove</u> the statement.

You will need:
Torch
Two square pieces of card
Scissors

1 Make a small hole in the exact centre of both pieces of card. Use a ruler to help you measure this!

2 Arrange the pieces of card so that they are 5cm apart with the holes in line.

3 Hold the torch 3cm from the first piece of card and switch it on.

4 Look through the hole in the second piece of card.

● Can you see the light? _____

● Move one of the cards out of line. Look through the hole in the second piece of card again.

● Can you see the light now? _____

● Why do you think that is?

_____

● How can you make sure this is a fair test and that your results can be trusted?

_____

A DOG'S DIARY 1

- Sir Isaac Newton was a famous scientist working in the 17th century. His work with forces is legendary – the rules he discovered still help us with designing cars, aeroplanes and football boots to this day!

- He also worked on light and made some more amazing discoveries ... as his not-so-smart doggy, Diamond, reveals exclusively to you today...

A dog's diary by Diamond

Cambridge ~ 2 June 1664

My master, Isaac is grumpy today. Oh well, so what – he's a miserable human. Mind you his bark is worse than his bite – ha ha. Actually, Isaac's mum is to blame. Isaac and I are at College but Isaac's skint. Isaac's mum is really rich but she never sends us any pocket money. So poor Isaac has to earn a few pennies by working as a waiter in the College. Then he's allowed to eat the scraps and leftovers. And guess what I get? Isaac's scraps and leftovers.
Oh well, it's a dog's life.

31 August

Isaac is barking mad. (Well mad, anyway.) We went to a fair but instead of buying a nice juicy joint of meat for me, Isaac spent his hard-earned pennies on a prism. Well, he calls it a "prism". I call it a stupid triangular lump of glass that you can't even eat. So I whimpered in protest.

Isaac looked down at me in surprise.
"Are you OK?" he asked.
My master often talks to me because he doesn't have too many human friends.
"I'm rough," I replied.
Actually it sounded more like "ruff!" so Isaac ignored me. Well, he's still working and I'm dog-tired. So I'm taking my grumbling belly off to bed.

Woolsthorpe, Lincolnshire ~ 25 December 1665

We're here staying with Isaac's mum. It's all to do with something called "the plague". Well, humans are dropping dead like flies and the College is closed. So we came here. It's a good thing this plague. Now I get fed regularly by Isaac's mum. Yum, yum – Christmas goose bones.

1 January 1666

My master missed supper ... again. As usual, he's up in his room scribbling masses of meaningless numbers and mumbling scientific gibberish about light. He never washes or changes his clothes – phwoar, he's really going to the dogs. Mind you, I'm always ready to help my master. That's why I made

A DOG'S DIARY 2

sure I was at hand to eat his supper for him. At least it didn't go to waste!

12 January
I sneaked into Isaac's room today. Got a bit of a shock. Isaac has made a small hole in the shutters. (I bet his mum will have a fit when she sees the damage.) A ray of light shone through the hole and made a blob of sunlight on the wall. This proves my theory – Isaac is completely bonkers.

13 January
Lovely crisp, sunny morning – perfect for walkies. So I bounded into Isaac's room joyfully barking and wagging my tail. And guess what I saw? A bright beam of sunlight shone through that funny hole and on to that useless glass prism. The light shone out of the prism and hit the wall and the wall was covered in colours. Weird. It looked like a rainbow.

Well, at first I thought "Cor – that's a neat bit of painting," but then I realized the colours

funny hole / prism / white light / rainbow

were made by the light. "Maybe that prism has magical powers," I thought.

Then I saw the broad grin on Isaac's face.

"What do you think of the rainbow, Diamond?" he whispered excitedly, pressing his face up close.

"Woof!" I replied. This is usually the best response when Isaac gets worked up about something.

"Bet you'd like to know how I made it?" asked Isaac.

Well, I was wondering and luckily he went on to explain the trick.

"You see, sunlight is made of different colours."

I wagged my tail and looked interested as Isaac continued in a rather breathless voice.

"When the colours in light hit the prism at an angle they all bend or refract by different amounts. So the colours separate out from the white light and you see a rainbow."

Well, all this Science was a bit over my head and anyway I was bursting for a pee. Luckily Isaac's mum heard me whining and she took me for walkies.

Ah – what a relief!

Diamond's disgrace!
Unfortunately Diamond is only known to us by his less clever deeds ... One Sunday, Isaac went to church leaving a candle in his laboratory.

Perhaps Diamond wanted to try a few experiments too. Anyway, he jumped on the table, knocked over the candle and started a fire. According to one report, the blaze destroyed all Isaac's notes on light and all his chemistry equipment. I expect poor Diamond ended up in the dog house.

NAME _____   DATE _____

- Take a good look at the prism and describe it.

- Let a ray of sunlight shine through the prism. What do you see?

_____

_____

_____

- Draw it here in full colour!

- Now try this experiment of Newton's.

- This time you use two prisms and a card with a narrow slit that only allows the red light through.

- Take a look at the diagram. What would happen to the light?

_____

_____

- What would be different about the light coming from prism 2?

_____

_____

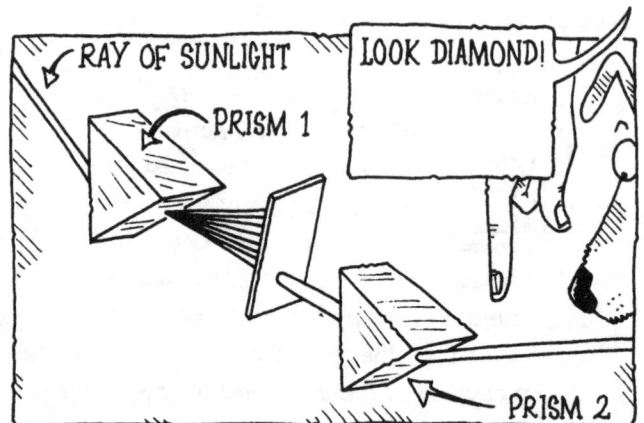

- Colour in this diagram accurately, using the correct colours.

- What do you think Isaac might have said to dim doggy Diamond? Write it in this speech bubble!

Bet you never knew!
Newton was the first person to describe seven colours in light, but actually there are lots more. Newton liked the idea of seven colours, though, because it reminded him of the seven notes in music.

NAME _____   DATE _____

The adventures of Super-Photon! 1

So light brightens up our lives. But take a closer look at light and it's even more fantastic. Imagine you could look at a ray of light through an incredibly powerful microscope. It would have to be billions of times more powerful than the world's most powerful microscope. Here's what you might see.

AH! LOVELY PHOTONS!

LIGHT IS MADE UP OF TINY BLIPS CALLED PHOTONS (FO-TONS).

PHOTON MAGNIFIED MILLIONS OF TIMES.

● But to really find out about what light is made up of you need to super-shrink yourself to the size of an atom. Atoms are so small that it would take more than a million to stretch across the *thickness* of this page! Everything in the universe is made up of billions and billions of them – even you! And **photons** are even smaller – but boy are they tough!

Meanwhile on Earth...

ARGH!

NOW I'VE GOT YOU AGENT BRIGHT!

THE EVIL PROFESSOR Z! LOOKS LIKE A JOB FOR SUPER-PHOTON!

Because just then...

NOT SO FAST, Z!

HA HA, PREPARE TO DIE.

1.25 seconds later...

A MIRROR? THAT WON'T STOP ME!

WHOOSH!

In a split second Super-Photon leaps clear of the sun and streaks towards the Earth at 300,000 km (186,000 miles) per second.

In just six minutes he flashes past Venus.

HI VENUS – BYE VENUS!

Super-Photon bounces off the mirror and dazzles the evil Professor.

ARGH! I CAN'T SEE!

IT'S SUPER-PHOTON!

DAZZLE!

Meanwhile back on Earth...

YOU WON'T GET AWAY WITH THIS, Z!

ANY LAST REQUESTS?

HAS TIME RUN OUT FOR AGENT BRIGHT?

Eight minutes and twenty-five seconds into his mission Super-Photon flashes past the moon. But is he too late?

GRRR! WHERE'S SHE GONE!

I'VE GOTTA GO!

THE END

NAME _____ DATE _____

The adventures of Super-Photon! 2

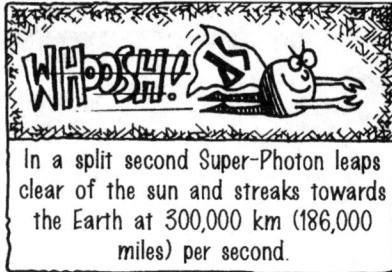

WHOOSH!

In a split second Super-Photon leaps clear of the sun and streaks towards the Earth at 300,000 km (186,000 miles) per second.

● Now it's time to adapt the cartoon into an action drama.

● Use this planner to help you.

Roles (and actors!)

Props (only use props that are really needed, you might be able to mime others – or use other actors to represent them!)

Music (try to include some good music to help get the action whizzing along!)

Ideas for the script (split the action into scenes to be acted in order, give your actors dialogue and stage directions so they know what to say and do. Write out your script on a separate piece of paper. Oh, try to use movement as much as possible to make it a true action drama!)

Costume designs (keep them simple so that your actors can move easily!)

Ideas for a poster (make it eye-catching to attract a good audience!)

Extra ideas (anything else you can think of?)

Bet you never knew!
1 Actually, there's nothing special about Super-Photon. The sun produces trillions of photons every second and there's nothing remarkable about Super-Photon's powers.
2 Every day thousands of billions of these tiny blips of energy travel 150,000,000km through the wastes of space just to whack you! But because photons don't weigh anything you don't feel them smacking into your head.
3 You might wonder what happens to photons after they hit something. Well, remember a photon is just a blip of energy. It hits an atom and its energy is soaked up. So it's bye-bye photon.

NAME _____   DATE _____

The adventures of Super-Photon! 3

HORRIBLE SCIENCE

PRESENTS

ZERO! Super-Photon weighs nothing at all. He's far too small to see, far smaller even than an atom.

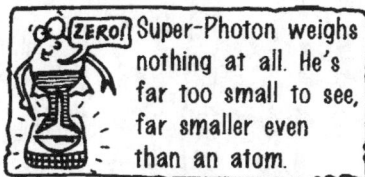

SCRIPTED BY, DIRECTED BY AND STARRING...

CLASS _____

Professor Buzzoff's great experiment-a-thon! 1

PICTURE THIS!

WHAT I NEEDED:

A MAGNIFYING GLASS

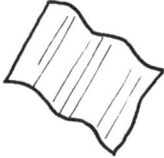

A WHITE A4 PIECE OF PAPER

A WINDOW WITH DARK CURTAINS AND A BRIGHT SUNNY DAY OUTSIDE

WHAT I DID:

1 I closed the curtains until only a thin stream of sunlight could get through.

2 I placed the paper on a table in front of the window.

3 Then I held the magnifying glass in front of the crack in the curtains and adjusted its position until light shone through the glass and on to the paper.

RESULT: A colour image of the view outside appeared on the paper - remarkable! I had to adjust the position of the glass, moving it a little nearer or a little further from the paper until the picture was in focus.

REMARKS: The lens of the magnifying glass bent the light coming from the scene outside on to the paper. The light was so bright that it made a picture.

PHANTOM FACE

WHAT YOU NEED:

A BRIGHT TORCH

A MIRROR

A FRIEND (ONE OF MY SCIENTIFIC COLLEAGUES HELPED ME).

WHAT YOU DO:

1 Wait until dark and make sure the curtains are open. Hide in a corner of the room opposite the window.

2 Ask your friend to hold the mirror so it reflects light on to the window. You can work this out by shining your torch on to the mirror and watching to see where the light reflects.

3 Shine the torch on to your face from below and pull a horrible face. Stand so that the light from your face reflects on to the mirror.

WHAT DID YOU NOTICE?

ANSWER: A ghostly face appears at the window - you'll probably spot it out of the corner of your eye. In fact, the light is reflected from your face to the mirror and from the mirror to the window and then back into the room.

FRIEND

ME

MOONIM

Professor Buzzoff's great experiment-a-thon! 2

MIXED-UP COLOURS

WHAT I NEEDED: SOME OLIVE OIL... A RULER

A JAM-JAR

SOME BLUE MOUTHWASH OR SOME WATER MIXED WITH THREE DROPS OF BLUE FOOD COLOUR

OIL

MOUTHWASH

WHAT I DID:

1 I poured enough mouthwash to fill the jar to a depth of 5 cm (2 inches).

2 Then I poured on a layer of olive oil 0.5 cm (0.2 inches) thick – the oil floated on the mouthwash.

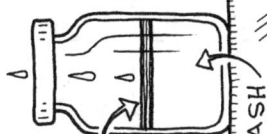

3 I replaced the lid of the jar and shook it well and held the liquid up to the light.

SHAKE!

GREEN!

RESULT: The liquid had turned green! After a few minutes, the yellow olive oil reappeared on top of the blue liquid.

REMARKS: Sunlight contains the colours in the rainbow. The colour of the oil and the mouthwash is due to their atoms only letting yellow and blue light through. When yellow and blue light is combined you get green light and that's why I saw green! John I have poured the mixture away but I left it lying around. I later mistook it for salad dressing and put it on my lettuce. YUCK!

THUMB SOME LIGHT

WHAT YOU NEED:

TWO THUMBS. (IT HELPS IF THEY'RE YOUR OWN.)

A LIGHT. (A BRIGHT WINDOW WILL DO)

WHAT YOU DO:

1 Put your thumbs together with the nails facing you. The thumbs should be just 3 mm (0.2 inches) apart.

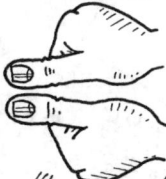

2 Bring your thumbs up so that you're looking at the light through the gap between your thumbs. They should be about 5 cm (2 inches) from your face.

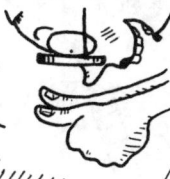

WHAT DID YOU NOTICE?

actually caused by light waves shining from different directions getting in each other's way and blotting each other out. I hope you like my drawing – it's rather artistic if I say so myself!

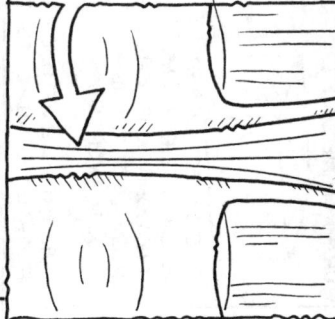

ANSWER: Thin lines appear between your thumbs. If you realized they were due to light you'll be on the right lines. (Sorry, that was a joke: just my artistic side trying to express itself!) The lines are

Professor Buzzoff's great experiment-a-thon! 3

A GHOST OF A CHANCE

WHAT I NEEDED:

A BOX AT LEAST 12 CM WIDE x 17.5 CM LONG x 12 CM HIGH (4.7 INCHES x 7 INCHES).

A POSTCARD-SIZED PICTURE OF A GRAVEYARD OR RUIN. (I CUT THIS OUT OF A MAGAZINE BUT BEING A BIT OF AN ARTIST I'M GOING TO PAINT MY OWN SCENE. IT HAS TO BE 17.5 CM LONG AND 12 CM HIGH TO FIT THE BOX.)

A THIN LENGTH OF WIRE (FLORIST'S WIRE IS IDEAL).

A RULER

SCISSORS

SOME WHITE PAPER

BLU-TAK

A PIECE OF STIFF CELLOPHANE AT LEAST 21 CM (8.3) LONG AND 10 CM (3.4 INCHES) HIGH

PENCIL

WHAT I DID:

1 I cut one of the long sides off the box, and 5 cm (2 inches) from one end I made a viewing window 2.5 cm (1 inch) square as shown.

2 I used Blu-tak to stick the picture on the inside wall of the box opposite the window.

3 I placed the Cellophane diagonally between the corners of the box and used Blu-tak to hold the Cellophane in place.

4 I drew a ghost shape on the paper 9 cm (3.5 inches) high and 2.5 cm (1 inch) across. Here's the shape I drew – told you I was a bit of an artist!

FRONT

BACK

5 I stuck a piece of wire to the ghost's head with blu-tak.

6 Now for the interesting bit! I shone a bright light on to the box from above

(actually this wasn't vital because I could have put the box by a window). Then holding the wire, I dangled the ghost inside the box through the open top. I looked through the viewing window and saw...

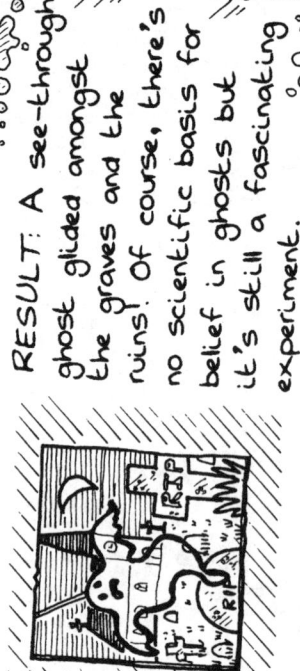

RESULT: A see-through ghost glided amongst the graves and the ruins! Of course, there's no scientific basis for belief in ghosts but it's still a fascinating experiment.

REMARKS: This illusion is known as Pepper's ghost after the Victorian scientist who invented it. The light reflected off the ghost shape and on to the Cellophane. The Cellophane was see-through or "transparent" as we scientists say, and this makes the reflection of the ghost appear transparent.

NAME _____   DATE _____

Professor Buzzoff's great experiment-a-thon discovery sheet!

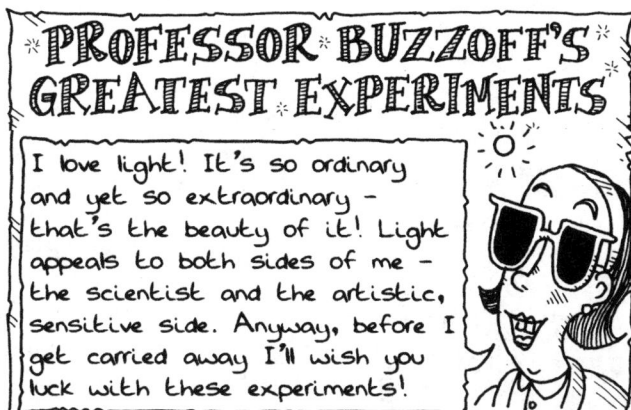

PROFESSOR BUZZOFF'S GREATEST EXPERIMENTS

I love light! It's so ordinary and yet so extraordinary – that's the beauty of it! Light appeals to both sides of me – the scientist and the artistic, sensitive side. Anyway, before I get carried away I'll wish you luck with these experiments!

Experiment 1: _____

Equipment we used: _____

What I discovered: _____

Experiment 2: _____

Equipment we used: _____

What I discovered: _____

Experiment 3: _____

Equipment we used: _____

What I discovered: _____

Experiment 4: _____

Equipment we used: _____

What I discovered: _____

Experiment 5: _____

Equipment we used: _____

What I discovered: _____

● Which was your favourite experiment and why? _____

_____

NAME _____   DATE _____

Frightening light quiz!

Without sunlight you can't see...
1 A rainbow. TRUE/FALSE

2 The moon. TRUE/FALSE

PREPARE
TO LAND...
ARGH!
WHERE'S
IT GONE?

If it's completely dark...
3 Your face wouldn't appear in a mirror. TRUE/FALSE

WITH A
FACE LIKE
THAT,
CAN YOU
BLAME IT?

4 You couldn't take holiday snaps. TRUE/FALSE

5 A poisonous rattlesnake couldn't find where you are hiding. TRUE/FALSE

RATTLE!
RATTLE!

PLEASE LET
IT BE TRUE,
PLEASE LET
IT BE TRUE...

Answers:
1 TRUE. A rainbow happens when sunlight shines through droplets of rain. This splits the sunlight into different colours. You actually get rainbows at night made by moonlight but the colours are too dim for your eyes to make out.
2 TRUE. The moon doesn't make its own light. That pretty silvery moonlight is actually sunlight that's bounced off (or as a scientist might say, reflected from) the moon. The surface of the moon is made of rock and dust but if it was ice it would reflect light really well and the moon would be nearly as bright as the sun.
3 TRUE. A mirror works by reflecting light. There's nothing to stop you looking at the bathroom mirror in the dark. But since there's no light the mirror won't reflect your image. Mind you, according to legend, if you're a vampire the mirror won't show your image anyway.
4 TRUE. Imagine you went pot-holing in a dark cave and left your torch at home. Whoops. You couldn't take any snaps because the chemicals that make a photograph only work if light falls on the film.
5 FALSE. The rattlesnake has a pit on each side of its head full of temperature sensors. These detect heat from your body. It's frightening. And that's why hiding from the snake in a dark cupboard isn't such a clever idea.

● Now use the internet and books to research your own horrible frightening light quiz questions!